Why We Give Gifts at Christmas Ti:

By Corine Hyman, Ph.D.

Illustrated by Julie Bryant

Teaching Christ's Children

Baltimore, Maryland 2012

Illustrations and Book Design by

Julie Bryant of sweetartdesign.com

ISBN 978-0-9855-423-9-9

Teaching Christ's Children

Baltimore, Maryland

2012

Dedication

May all the glory and honor go to the
Savior and Lord of the world, Jesus Christ.

Hello, my name is Evelyn and these are my friends.

Jesus is the reason
for our Christmas season

We have been learning about why we give gifts to others at Christmas time even though it is Jesus' birthday.

This is my friend Sarah. Hi Sarah. Hey Sarah can you tell me why you give gifts at Christmas time?

I love giving gifts at Christmas time and throughout the year because it reminds me of God giving me the gift of His only son. Because of God's gift, I know I will one day live forever.

There is my friend, Jayden. Hey Jayden, what did you learn about why we give gifts at Christmas time?

I learned when I give gifts at Christmas time and throughout the year to do it with a cheerful spirit because I know it will please God.

2 Corinthians 9:7 Each of you should give as you have decided in your heart to give. You should not be sad when you give, and you should not give because you feel forced to give. God loves the person who gives happily. (NCV)

This is my friend Madison. Hello Madison. Why do you give gifts at Christmas time?

Hello Evelyn. I give gifts at Christmas time to my family and friends because I know it pleases my Lord and Savior.

Acts 20:35 Jesus said; "It is more blessed to give than to receive." (NIV)

This is my friend Isabella. Hello Isabella. What did you learn about giving gifts?

Hey Evelyn, I learned that when I receive gifts, I should share them with others. This will please my Heavenly Father.

Numbers 10:32 We will share with you all the good things the Lord gives us. (NIV)

There is Christopher. Hello Christopher. Who do you give gifts to at Christmas time and throughout the year?

I give gifts to those that have less than me. I can do this by working in a soup kitchen or giving some of my toys to other children. When I do these things, I will show other people that Jesus cares about them and I do too.

Romans 12:13 Share with God's people who need help. Practice hospitality. (NIV)

Here is Grace. Hi Grace, Christopher told me he gives gifts to people who have less than him.

I also give gifts to people who have less than me because when I do I am not really giving to people but to God.

Blankets

Matthew 25:40 Then the King will answer, "I tell you the truth, anything you did for even the least of my people here, you also did for me." (NCV)

This is my friend, Chaya. Hello Chaya. Please tell me why you give gifts at Christmas time.

I give gifts at Christmas time because my Heavenly Father has given me spiritual gifts. My spiritual gift is helping others. I help my mommy with my baby brother a lot. My mommy says teaching is her spiritual gift which is why she teaches our Sunday school class. She also says there are many other spiritual gifts like . . . giving and preaching. When you use your spiritual gifts you make God happy. I try to use my spiritual gift as much as I can.

1 Corinthians 7:7 Each person has his own gift from God. One has one gift, another has another gift. (NCV)

Well Evelyn, right now I am little and do not have much. But what I have I will share with others because I know God will be pleased.

Hebrews 13:16 Do not forget to do good to others, and share with them, because such sacrifices please God. (NCV)

I learned when I give a gift to expect nothing in return. I am giving my friend Eryn a birthday gift even though she did not give me a birthday gift.

Matthew 10:8 Freely you have received, freely give. (NIV)

Hey there is my friend, Michael. Hello Michael, what can you tell me about giving gifts at Christmas time?

When I give gifts at Christmas time and throughout the year, I will not only give stuff but I will give my time as well.

1 Chronicles 29:14 *Everything comes from you; we have given you back what you gave us. (NIV)*

There is my friend Efrem. Hello Efrem. Why do you give gifts at Christmas time?

I give gifts at Christmas time and throughout the year to God because all that I have God gave to me.

1 Chronicles 29:14 Everything comes from you; we have given you back what you gave us. (NCV)

And me? Are you wondering what I learned?

Well I learned to give gifts at Christmas time and throughout the year because Christ freely gave me the gift of salvation when he died for my sins.

Ephesians 2:8-9 For by grace are ye saved through faith; and that not of yourselves: it is the gift of God: Not of works, lest any man should boast. (NIV)

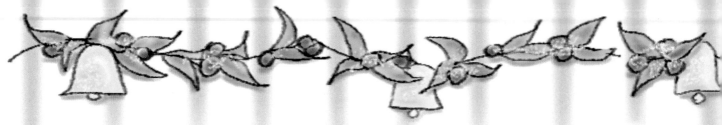

You see, even though it is Jesus' birthday, we will give gifts at Christmas time and throughout the year for all these reasons and many more.

Why will you give gifts this year?

The Christmas Story
Luke 2:1-20(NCV)

The Birth of Jesus

2 At that time, Augustus Caesar sent an order that all people in the countries under Roman rule must list their names in a register. 2 This was the first registration; it was taken while Quirinius was governor of Syria. 3 And all went to their own towns to be registered. 4 So Joseph left Nazareth, a town in Galilee, and went to the town of Bethlehem in Judea, known as the town of David. Joseph went there because he was from the family of David. 5 Joseph registered with Mary, to whom he was engaged and who was now pregnant. 6 While they were in Bethlehem, the time came for Mary to have the baby, 7 and she gave birth to her first son. Because there were no rooms left in the inn, she wrapped the baby with pieces of cloth and laid him in a feeding trough.

Shepherds Hear About Jesus

8 That night, some shepherds were in the fields nearby watching their sheep. 9 Then an angel of the Lord stood before them. The glory of the Lord was shining around them, and they became very frightened. 10 The angel said to them, "Do not be afraid. I am bringing you good news that will be a great joy to all the people. 11 Today your Savior was born in the town of David. He is Christ, the Lord. 12 This is how you will know him: You will find a baby wrapped in pieces of cloth and lying in a feeding box." 13 Then a very large group of angels from heaven joined the first angel, praising God and saying: 14 "Give glory to God in heaven, and on earth let there be peace among the people who please God."   15 When the angels left them and went back to heaven, the shepherds said to each other, "Let's go to Bethlehem. Let's see this thing that has happened which the Lord has told us about." 16 So the shepherds went quickly and found Mary and Joseph and the baby, who was lying in a feeding trough. 17 When they had seen him, they told what the angels had said about this child. 18 Everyone was amazed at what the shepherds said to them.   19 But Mary treasured these things and continued to think about them.   20 Then the shepherds went back to their sheep, praising God and thanking him for everything they had seen and heard. It had been just as the angel had told them.

Made in United States
Orlando, FL
08 December 2022

25802314R00020